MARKET STRUCTURE TOP DOWN ANALYSIS

A Comprehensive Approach To Forex Market Analysis

JIDE GEORGE

Copyright © 2024 Jide George

All rights reserved. No part of this book may be reproduced, distributed, or transmitted in any form or by any means, including photocopying, recording, or other electronic or mechanical methods, without the prior written permission of the author, except in the case of brief quotations embodied in critical reviews and certain other noncommercial uses permitted by copyright law. For permission requests, please contact the author.

TABLE OF CONTENT

Introduction _____ *11*

Chapter 1 _____ *17*

  The Forex Trader's Journey _____ 17

    Key Features of a Structured Approach: _____ 19

    Key Elements of Market Structure _____ 20

Chapter 2 _____ *23*

  Understanding Market Structure _____ 23

    Support & Resistance _____ 24

    Trends _____ 26

    Ranges _____ 28

Chapter 3 _____ *32*

  The Power of Top-Down Analysis _____ 32

    Define Top-Down Analysis _____ 33

    Advantages of a Hierarchical Approach _____ 33

    Overview of Timeframes _____ 34

Chapter 4 _____ *40*

  Starting from the top: Monthly and weekly charts. _____ 40

    Identifying long-term trends. _____ 40

      The Best Way to Identify Long-Term Trends _____ 41

      Weekly Chart Analysis: Key Points _____ 41

      Identifying Major Support and Resistance Levels _____ 42

How to Identify Major Levels _____ 42

Case Study: How Major Economic Events Influence Long-Term Charts __ 43

Practical Use of Monthly and Weekly Analysis _____ 44

   Determine Your Bias _____ 44

   Identify key levels _____ 44

   Understand momentum _____ 44

   Patience is key _____ 45

Chapter 5 _____ 48

Zooming in on daily and 4-hour charts _____ 48

Intermediate Trend Analysis _____ 48

How to Effectively Use 4-Hour Charts _____ 49

Spotting Key Swing Highs and lows _____ 50

The Art of Drawing Trendlines _____ 51

   How to Draw Effective Trend Lines _____ 51

Practical Use of Daily and 4-Hour Analysis _____ 52

   Identify Entry Points _____ 52

   Set Realistic Targets _____ 52

   Manage risk _____ 52

   Spot Divergences _____ 53

   Monitor Multiple Pairs _____ 53

Chapter 6 _____ 56

One-Hour and Lower Timeframes _____ 56

Short-term Market Structure _____ 56

Ensure precise entry and exit points _____ 58

Balancing Big Picture and Immediate Opportunities _____ 58

Practical Applications of Short-Term Analysis _____ 59

Chapter 7 _____ 64

Price Action Patterns and Market Structure _____ 64

Candlestick Patterns That Matter _____ 64

Doji _____ 65

Engulfing patterns _____ 65

Pin Bars _____ 67

Chart Patterns: The Overall Picture _____ 69

Double Tops and Bottoms _____ 69

Triangles Pattern: _____ 70

Flags and Pennants _____ 71

Understanding how patterns fit into the larger market structure _____ 72

Practical Use of Price Action Patterns _____ 73

Entry Timing _____ 73

Placement of Stop Losses _____ 73

Take Profit Levels _____ 73

Failure Patterns _____ 74

Pattern Confluence _____ 74

Chapter 8 _____ 78

Volume and Market Structure _____ 78

Volume Confirms Trends _____ 78

Volume Spread Analysis Basics _____ 79

Adding Volume to Your Top-Down Approach _____ 80

Begin with longer timeframes _____ 80

Move to daily charts _____ 80

Fine-tune using intraday charts _____ 81

Practical Application of Volume Analysis _____ 81

   Trend Confirmation _____ 81

   Breakout Trading _____ 81

   Support and Resistance _____ 82

   Divergences _____ 82

   Climactic Action _____ 82

Chapter 9 _____ *86*

Fundamental Analysis within the Framework of Market Structure 86

   How Economic Events Impact Market Structure _____ 86

   Aligning Fundamental Outlook and Technical Structure _____ 88

   Case studies on major fundamental shifts and their technical implications
_____ 89

      Case Study #1: Brexit Vote (2016) _____ 89

         Fundamental Impact _____ 89

         Technical Implication _____ 89

         Lesson _____ 89

      Case Study 2: Fed Rate Hike Cycle (2015–2018) _____ 89

         Fundamental impact _____ 89

         Technical Implication _____ 89

         Lesson _____ 90

      Case Study #3: COVID-19 Pandemic (2020) _____ 90

         Fundamental Impact: _____ 90

         Technical Implication _____ 90

         Lesson _____ 90

   Practical Use of Fundamental Analysis in Market Structure: _____ 90

Chapter 10 — *94*

Trading with the trend — **94**

Determining the path of least resistance — 94

Methods for identifying trends — 95

Strategies for Trend Continuation Trading — 96

Entry confirmation techniques: — 97

Risk management tips: — 98

Practical Applications of Trend Trading — 98

Chapter 11 — *102*

Mastering range-bound markets. — **102**

Recognize Consolidation Phases. — 102

Key range identification techniques: — 103

Strategies for trading ranges — 103

Breakout Trading: From Ranges to Trends — 104

Strategies for Breakout Trading — 105

Practical Application of Range Trading — 105

Chapter 12 — *110*

The Art of Confluence — **110**

Combining many timeframes — 110

Key Multi-Timeframe Techniques — 111

    Trend Alignment — 111

    Support/Resistance Confluence — 111

    Entry Confirmation — 111

Finding Agreement Between Indicators and Price Action. — 112

Strategies for Indicator Confluence — 112

Creating a Confluence checklist _____ 113

Practical Applications of Confluence _____ 114

Chapter 13 _____ 118

Risk Management and Position Sizing _____ 118

Analyzing Market Structures to Protect Your Capital _____ 118

    Identify key levels _____ 118

    Recognize Volatility _____ 118

    Recognize potential reversals _____ 118

Setting stop losses based on structure _____ 119

Stop-loss strategies _____ 120

Position Sizing Strategies for Various Market Conditions _____ 120

Tips for position sizing _____ 121

Practical Application of Risk Management _____ 121

    Pre-Trade Checklist _____ 121

    Risk/Reward Ratio _____ 121

    Drawdown Rules _____ 122

    Regularly review your trades _____ 122

    Before entering a trade _____ 122

    Emotional Control _____ 122

Chapter 14 _____ 126

Building Your Trading Plan _____ 126

Incorporate Market Structure Analysis into Your Daily Routine _____ 126

Develop a Top-Down Analysis Template _____ 127

Practical Applications of Your Trading Plan _____ 129

Chapter 15 _____ 134

Advanced Concepts of Market Structure — 134

Order Flow and Market Structure — 134
- Identify Key Levels: — 134
- Spotting Reversals: — 134
- Understanding Momentum — 135

Important order flow concepts — 135

Using Market Profile and Structure Analysis — 135

Market Profile Applications — 136
- Identify Fair Value — 136
- Spot Failed Moves — 136
- Understand Trader mood — 136

Fibonacci Levels and Their Impact on Market Structure — 136

Trading Methods Using Fibonacci — 137

Practical use of advanced concepts — 137
- Begin slowly — 138
- Demonstrate the techniques — 138
- Combine with Basics — 138
- Be selective — 138
- Continuous Learning — 138
- Seek Mentorship — 138

Chapter 16 — 142

The Future Of Forex Trading — 142

Analysis of emerging technologies in the market. — 142
- AI and Machine Learning — 142
- Big Data Analytics — 142
- Blockchain and Cryptocurrencies — 143

Considerations for new technologies _____ 143
Responding to shifting market dynamics. _____ 143
    Global Economic Shifts _____ 144
    Evolving trading instruments _____ 144
    Changing trading hours _____ 144
Tips for responding to market changes _____ 144
Continuous learning and improvement _____ 145
Strategies for Continuous Improvement _____ 145
Practical Application to Future-Proof Your Trading _____ 146

Conclusion _____ *150*

Introduction

The Forex Market It's a world where riches can be created and lost in the blink of an eye, where the timid fear to tread, and where the brave might seize unrivaled possibilities. But make no mistake: this isn't a place for the inexperienced or reckless. It's a battleground where knowledge is power, and strategy reigns supreme.

You've probably heard the stories about the newbie trader who made a fortune on their first trade, or the seasoned pro who lost everything in a market crash. These stories may lead you to believe that forex trading is all about luck or a mysterious sixth sense. But believe me when I say it isn't. It is important to comprehend the market's DNA, its very structure, and this is where market structure top-down analysis comes in.

Now you may be wondering, "What the heck is market structure top-down analysis?" It's like having the skills of a psychologist, scientist, and investigator all rolled into one, my friend.

It's about peeling back the layers of the market, beginning with the big picture and working your way down to the smallest elements. It is a thorough approach that investigates every possible avenue.

I've been in the trenches for years, monitoring the charts and understanding the trends, and trust me, this strategy has saved my skin more times than I can count. It's more than just staring at lovely lines on a graph. It is about understanding the market's psychology, habits, and quirks. It's about viewing the forest and trees and understanding how they relate to one another.

Imagine the currency market as a large ocean. Waves and ripples are visible on the surface, but beneath them are currents and undercurrents that influence one another. Top-down analysis is analogous to diving deep into these seas, understanding how the tides work, how the currents move, and how they all interact to form the patterns we see on the surface.

However, the most important part is that it's not merely about analyzing. It is about synthesis. It's about gathering all of this knowledge and organizing it into a clear approach.

It's about understanding when to ride the wave and when to go under it. It's about realizing that sometimes the best trade is none at all.

You see, many traders become engrossed in the details. They are so fixated on the 5-minute chart that they overlook the weekly trend. They are so focused on the next trade that they forget about risk management. It's like attempting to navigate the ocean by staring at a puddle. Top-down analysis provides perspective. It allows you to view the big picture without losing track of the specifics.

But let's go honest for a moment. This is not a get-rich-quick program. It's not a secret strategy that will make you a forex millionaire overnight. It's a strong tool, but its effectiveness is determined by how you utilize it. It demands perseverance, discipline, and a desire to learn. It requires that you leave your ego at the door and be willing to confess when you're wrong.

I've watched traders come and go. I've witnessed people ride high on a lucky streak, only to crash and burn when the market turns against them. However, the ones that stick around and genuinely flourish are those who understand market structure.

They are the ones who take a top-down approach, viewing the market as a complex, dynamic system that necessitates ongoing study and modification.

In this book, we'll go deeply into the subject of market structure top-down analysis. We'll begin with the fundamentals, laying a strong foundation of knowledge. Then we'll step up and look at how to apply these principles in real-world trading circumstances. We'll look at charts in a variety of timeframes, from monthly to hourly. We'll examine at how fundamentals and technicals interact, how volume influences price movement, and how to properly manage risk.

But more importantly, we'll learn how to think like a good forex trader. We'll cultivate the attitude required to traverse the turbulent waters of the currency markets. We'll learn to be patient when the market requires it, and resolute when it's time to take action. We'll learn to be adaptable, shifting our strategies as the market changes.

This road will not be easy. There will be hurdles, disappointments, and periods of uncertainty. But this is the nature of forex trading.

It requires a certain level of courage. It is for people who are willing to put in the effort, who want to learn and grow, and who are prepared to face and overcome their concerns.

So, are you prepared to take your forex trading to the next level? Are you prepared to perceive the market in a completely new light? Are you prepared to learn the art and science of market structure top-down analysis? If that's the case, then buckle up. We are about to start on a trip that will permanently transform the way you trade. Let's plunge in and discover the secrets of the FX market together.

Chapter 1

The Forex Trader's Journey

The alarm goes off at 4:30 a.m. I get out of bed, my mind already racing with potential trades. This isn't just another day; it's a battlefield where fortunes are made and destroyed. Welcoming you to the world of foreign exchange trading.

You might believe we're all adrenaline addicts, addicted to screens and making split-second decisions. Sure, there's thrill, but successful trading doesn't require continual action. It requires patience, discipline, and a disciplined approach.

Let us break down an average day:

5:00 AM: Market overview. I begin by scanning the major currency pairs. What happened overnight? Is there any significant news? I'm not just looking at price changes; I'm looking for patterns and attempting to grasp the market's sentiment.

6:00 AM: Analysis time. Here's where the real work starts. I go into the charts, working my way down from monthly to hourly. It's like assembling a puzzle, with each timeframe providing a unique perspective.

- Monthly charts provide a comprehensive overview of market trends throughout time.
- Weekly charts show intermediate patterns and important levels.
- Daily charts show potential entry and exit points.
- Used 4-hour and 1-hour charts to improve my analysis.

7:30 A.M.: Plan Formulation Based on my analysis, I devise a trading strategy for the day. Which couples am I watching? What are my entrance and exit points? Where will I put my stop loss? This is not gambling; it is strategic planning.

Active trading hours are 8:00 AM to 4:00 PM. The markets are currently in full swing. But here's a secret: I don't continually trade. Most of my day is spent watching and waiting for the proper opportunity. When an opportunity matches with my strategy, I take action. Otherwise, I maintain patience.

4:00 PM - 5:00 PM: Review and Journal As the day finishes down, I examine my trades. What worked? What did not? I keep a notebook of every decision and emotion. This self-reflection is essential for development.

You know, successful forex trading does not mean generating money every day. It's about being consistent over time. The goal is to manage risk and preserve capital. Some days you win, some days you lose, but you're heading in the correct path.

Now, let's discuss the significance of an organized approach. Without structure, you're simply gambling. With structure, you are a professional.

Key Features of a Structured Approach:

- Establishing a consistent daily routine is essential for success.
- Analysis Framework: A systematic approach to evaluating the market over various time periods.
- Risk Management: Establish guidelines for position sizing and stop losses.
- Emotional Control: Techniques for managing the psychological aspects of trading.

- Practice continuous learning by reviewing and adapting your tactics.

This systematic approach is what distinguishes professionals from novices. It's not sexy or thrilling, but it works.

Let's delve deeper into market structure analysis, the foundation of my trading strategy.

Market structure is the framework that supports all price fluctuations. It's important to grasp support and resistance levels, trends, and ranges. But it goes beyond simply sketching lines on a chart. It's about comprehending the psychology underlying these moves.

Consider the market to be a huge swarm of dealers. Market structure analysis allows you to better comprehend the collective psychology of this audience. Are they optimistic or pessimistic? Are they confident or uncertain? Understanding this enables you to make better educated selections.

Key Elements of Market Structure:

- Support and Resistance: Price levels where the market has previously reversed. These are psychological impediments for traders.

- Trends refer to the overall direction of price change. The direction of a trend might be either upward, downward, or sideways.
- Range refers to price movement between two levels without a breakout.
- Breakouts occur when prices go beyond established support or resistance levels.

Understanding these components is critical, but the true strength comes from studying them over multiple timeframes. Here is when top-down analysis comes into play.

Top-down analysis begins with the overall picture and goes down to lesser timeframes. It's similar to looking at a map; you start with the overall view, then zoom into the state, city, and finally street level.

This technique provides context. It allows you to comprehend not only what the market is doing, but why it is doing it. It aligns your short-term trades with long-term patterns, which increases your chances of success.

Remember that forex trading is more like a marathon than a sprint. It necessitates dedication, lifelong learning, and a readiness to adapt.

The journey of a forex trader is difficult, but those who persevere can reap enormous rewards.

Are you prepared to upgrade your trading? Are you willing to put in the effort, develop the discipline, and master the art and science of Forex trading? Let us embark on this journey together, unraveling the market's mysteries one at a time.

Chapter 2

Understanding Market Structure

Let's go to the core of FX trading: market structure. It serves as the basis for successful trades, the unseen structure that influences price fluctuations. You may be pondering, "What makes this so important?" Understanding market structure chart is like to having a map in unfamiliar terrain. It helps you spot possibilities, directs your actions, and saves you from falling over a cliff.

So, what precisely is the market structure? It is fundamentally concerned with the ordering of price fluctuations throughout time. It refers to the market's patterns, rhythms, ebbs, and flows. However, it is more than simply squiggly lines on a chart. It reflects mass psychology and represents the combined activities of thousands of traders throughout the globe.

Let us break down the important elements:

Support & Resistance

These are the fundamentals of market structure. Support is a price level when buying pressure outweighs selling pressure, leading the price to increase. Resistance is the inverse - a level where selling pressure outweighs buying pressure, causing the price to fall.

Consider support as a floor, and resistance as a ceiling. But here's the catch: these levels are not set in stone. They may be broken, which often leads to big price fluctuations when they are.

How to Recognize Resistance and Support:

- Look for areas where price has repeatedly reversed
- Pay attention to round numbers (like 1.3000 in EUR/USD)
- Use technical indicators like Fibonacci retracements

Trends

A trend is the overall direction in which the market is going. It's like a river: it might flow up (bullish trend), down (bearish trend), or sideways (ranging market).

It is crucial to recognize trends because, as the phrase goes, "the trend is your friend." Trading with the trend improves your chances of success.

Trends Come in Many Forms:

- Uptrend with higher highs and lows.

- Downtrend with lower highs and lows

- Sideways: Price oscillates within a range, with no obvious direction.

Ranges

When the market isn't trending, it usually ranges. This occurs when the price swings between support and resistance levels without breaking out. Ranges might be unpleasant for trend traders, but they can provide opportunities.

Trading ranges necessitates a different approach. You want to buy around support and sell near resistance, rather than following a trend.

Chart patterns

These are distinct formations shown on price charts. They're basically the market's method of signaling its next move. Some frequent patterns include:

- Head and shoulders.
- Double tops and bottoms.
- Triangles (ascending, descending, and symmetrical)
- Flags and pennants

Each pattern has unique implications for future price fluctuations. Learning how to spot them may offer you a huge advantage.

Let's talk about the psychology of market structure now. This is when things get extremely fascinating.

Price levels and patterns are just one aspect of market structure. It is about human conduct on a grand scale. It is about fear, greed, hope, and despair. Each swing, trend, and pattern is the consequence of thousands of choices made by traders all across the globe.

When you look at a chart, you don't only observe price changes. You are seeing a war between buyers and sellers, bulls and bears. Support levels occur when traders perceive prices are low and start buying. Resistance arises when traders believe prices are too high and start selling.

Understanding this psychology is crucial. It helps you predict market changes rather than just react to them. For example, if the price approaches a high resistance level, you should expect many traders to sell. But if the price breaks past that resistance, those same traders may panic and buy back in, triggering more price increases.

This is the point where the concept of "smart money" enters in. These are the main players: institutional investors, central banks, and major trading businesses. They have the ability to shift markets, and understanding market structure may help you spot their imprints.

Have you ever witnessed prices abruptly revert after breaking a critical level? That might be clever money manipulating the market, driving away lesser traders before the big move occurs.

Now, let's talk about how you can use this information to your trading:

Determine Key Levels: Set your entrance and exit points using support and resistance. These levels are often the starting point for large movements.

Trade with the Trend: During an uptrend, seek for buying opportunities. Look for selling opportunity during a decline. Do not oppose the market.

Respect market ranges: by buying around support and selling near resistance. But prepare for a breakout.

Use several timeframes: The market structure on a daily chart may vary from a 1-hour chart. Using different periods provides a more full view.

Watch for Breakouts: Price frequently leads to a large move when it breaches a critical level. But be wary of fake outbreaks.

Understand Context: An uptrend's support level is stronger than one in a downtrend. Context is important.

Remember that market structure is not about forecasting the future. It is all about understanding probability. It's all about placing the odds in your favor.

As your trading career progresses, you'll start to see market structure everywhere. You'll spot level developing, recognize significant patterns, and grasp the ebb and flow of the market. It's like acquiring a sixth sense.

But do not get overconfident. The market might always surprise you. Risk management is crucial because of this. Even with a complete understanding of market structure, you will never win every trade. But you can change the odds in your favor.

In the next chapter, we'll look at how to use this understanding of market structure in a top-down analytical manner. We'll learn how to zoom out, view the broad picture, and then dig down to identify high-probability trading opportunities.

Remember that mastering market structure is a journey rather than a destination. Continue studying, watching, and, most importantly, trading. The market is the most effective instructor.

Chapter 3

The Power of Top-Down Analysis

Your forex battlefield secret weapon is top-down analysis. It is a process that converts the market's turmoil into an organized, manageable framework. Consider it your personal market GPS, directing you through the twists and turns of currency changes.

So, what precisely constitutes top-down analysis? It is fundamentally a hierarchical method to understanding market movements. You start with the large picture and gradually zoom in on the little elements. It's like looking at a forest, then trees, then leaves, and eventually veins within each leaf.

Let's break down the major components of top-down analysis:

Define Top-Down Analysis

Top-down analysis starts with the broadest perspective available. In forex, this entails beginning with long-term charts - monthly or even yearly. From then, you gradually shift to shorter timeframes: weekly, daily, 4-hour, 1-hour, and occasionally even less.

The attractiveness of this technique stems from its capacity to give context. Starting with the large picture helps you comprehend the general market attitude. This information then influences your analysis of shorter-term fluctuations.

Advantages of a Hierarchical Approach

Why bother with all of these timeframes? Can't you simply choose one and stick to it? You could, but you'd miss out on important information. Here's why a hierarchical strategy is so effective:

- Analyze several timeframes to verify trades fit with market trends. Trading with the trend improves your chances of success.
- Confirm support and resistance. A level that seems small on a 1-hour chart may be a crucial pivot point

on a weekly chart. Top-down analysis allows you to find the most critical levels.
- Optimize entry and departure points using lesser timeframes, while greater timeframes provide a comprehensive overview.
- Understanding market structure improves risk management by allowing for more effective stop losses and take profits.

Overview of Timeframes

Let's look more closely at what each timeframe can tell you.

- Monthly charts highlight long-term patterns and key support/resistance levels. They're like the market's tectonic plates: slow moving yet extremely strong.
- Weekly charts highlight intermediate trends and major swing moments. Weekly charts frequently indicate patterns that are imperceptible on shorter timeframes.
- Many traders begin their analysis using daily charts. Daily charts provide an appropriate mix between the overall picture and short-term fluctuations.

- 4-Hour charts are useful for detecting short-term trends and possible entry points.
- One-Hour Charts and Below: These timeframes are important for adjusting entry and maintaining open positions.

Now, you may be thinking, "That's a lot of charts to analyze!" And you're correct. Top-down analysis demands work. However, the insights it offers are worth every second.

Let's look at a realistic example:

Imagine you're looking at the EUR/USD currency pair. On the monthly chart, you can see a long-term uptrend. This is your first piece of information: the general market bias is bullish.

Zooming in on the weekly chart, you can see a retreat inside the uptrend. It's approaching a former resistance level, which might now serve as support. This might be a buying opportunity.

The daily chart shows a bullish candlestick pattern emerging at this support level. Your conviction increases.

Finally, you examine the 4-hour and 1-hour charts to choose an exact entry moment, maybe waiting for a breakout over a short-term resistance level.

Notice how each timeframe adds a layer of information? This is the power of top-down analysis.

However, it is important to understand that timeframes can occasionally contradict. The monthly chart may show an uptrend, while the daily chart shows a downtrend. This is not a weakness in the system; it is vital information. It indicates that the market is approaching a tipping point. In such cases, patience is essential. Before making a move, wait for the timeframes to match.

Now, let's speak about how to include top-down analysis into your trading practice.

- Begin analysis sessions with the broadest timeframe. Get a sense of the overall picture before delving into the minutiae.
- Check for Alignment: As you procced down timeframes, seek for confirmation of what you saw on upper timeframes. When numerous timeframes coincide, you've discovered a high-probability scenario.

- Use higher timeframes for direction and lower for entry: Higher timeframes indicate whether to buy or sell. Use shorter timeframes to improve your entry point.
- Don't Neglect Any Timeframe: Every degree of analysis adds value. Skipping a timeframe may result in losing critical information.
- Be patient. Top-down analysis frequently shows that the wisest course of action is to do nothing. Sometimes the most beneficial thing you can do is to wait for a better opportunities
- Regularly update your analysis. Markets change. Whatever was valid the previous week may not be valid today. Make top-down analysis a consistent aspect of your trading strategy.

One of the most significant advantages of top-down analysis is how it influences your trading mindset. Starting with the larger view helps you acquire perspective. What about the big swings on the 5-minute chart? They appear a lot less frightening when seen in the context of a robust weekly uptrend.

This strategy also helps you avoid one of the most common dangers in forex trading: overtrading.

Understanding the bigger market structure reduces your susceptibility to short-term changes. You'll have the courage to persist with your analysis and wait for high-probability settings.

Remember that top-down analysis is not about forecasting every market move. It's about understanding the market's structure and adapting to it. Increasing your chances of success is the key.

As you apply this strategy, you'll begin to perceive the market in a completely new perspective. Patterns will develop that you have never seen before. You will begin to anticipate market movements rather than just reacting to them.

But do not anticipate perfection. Even after a careful analysis, the market might surprise you. That is why integrating top-down analysis with effective risk management is critical. Use this strategy to identify profitable trades, but always protect your funds.

Chapter 4

Starting from the top: Monthly and weekly charts.

When you open your trading software and see a sea of candlesticks, where should you start? The answer lies in a larger perspective. Monthly and weekly charts serve as your compass in the enormous currency ocean. They indicate the currents that drive long-term price changes, laying the groundwork for all future trading decisions.

Let's explore the field of high-timeframe analysis:

Identifying long-term trends.

Monthly charts are the undisputed masters of trend detection. These charts condense a month's trading activity into a single candle, cutting through the clutter of daily changes.

The Best Way to Identify Long-Term Trends

- To identify an uptrend, look for higher highs and lower lows, and vice versa for a downtrend.
- Use moving averages. A 12-month and 24-month moving average crossover might indicate significant trend changes.
- Consider the angle of the trend: Steeper angles frequently signal greater trends.

I always start my analysis with a monthly chart. It's like taking a step back and seeing the whole jungle. You might be surprised at how often the market follows these long-term trends.

Weekly charts provide a bridge between the big-picture monthly view and the more granular daily charts. They are great at recognizing intermediate trends inside bigger monthly changes.

Weekly Chart Analysis: Key Points:

- Compare weekly and monthly trends. Are they in agreement or conflicting?
- Look for reversal patterns that may indicate the end of a long-term trend.

- Use weekly charts to better comprehend market direction.

Identifying Major Support and Resistance Levels

High-timeframe charts are excellent at displaying the most critical support and resistance levels. These are price points where the market has continuously reversed, often for years or even decades.

How to Identify Major Levels:

- Identify pricing zones that have been tried several times.
- Pay attention to psychological round figures, such as 1.0000 in EUR/USD.
- Use Fibonacci retracements to identify probable reversal points during significant swings.

These significant levels typically function as magnets, drawing pricing towards them. When price reaches a critical level on the monthly or weekly chart, take great attention.

Remember that support and resistance are zones rather than specific prices. These zones tend to be broader at high timeframes. On monthly charts, don't anticipate exactitude.

Case Study: How Major Economic Events Influence Long-Term Charts

Let's discuss how real-world events appear on high-timeframe charts. These charts reflect economic swings, political upheavals, and global catastrophes.

Consider the 2008 financial crisis as an example. The monthly chart of USD/JPY shows a huge fall that began in August 2008. This was more than simply a short-term volatility; it represented market pricing for a fundamental shift in the global economy.

Consider the Brexit vote in 2016. The GBP/USD monthly chart indicates a significant decrease in June 2016, followed by several months of negative pressure. These are not random movements; they reflect the market's long-term reaction to a significant political event.

Understanding the linkages between events and chart movements provides insight into how the forex market operates on a macro basis.

Practical Use of Monthly and Weekly Analysis

Now that we've covered the theory, let's speak about how to apply this knowledge in your trading:

Determine Your Bias: Use monthly charts to figure out your overall market bias. Are you normally optimistic or bearish about a currency pair?

Identify key levels: Mark the important support and resistance levels on your monthly and weekly charts. These will be useful reference points for all of your trading selections.

Understand momentum: The slope of long-term trends provides an indication of market momentum. Steep trends imply significant momentum, whilst flat trends may signal a probable reversal.

Plan Long-Term Trades: Monthly and weekly trade charts are your greatest friends if you're a position trader. They help you arrange trades that might last weeks or even months.

When using daily or 4-hour charts, remember to include monthly and weekly analysis. It gives important background for short-term fluctuations.

Patience is key: High-timeframe trading necessitates patience. Do not expect to locate trading opportunity every day. Prioritizing quality above quantity is key in this context.

One of the most significant benefits of focusing on monthly and weekly charts is the way it affects your trading psyche. When you zoom out and look at the broad picture, those alarming daily fluctuations become far less relevant.

It's like being on a boat on a turbulent sea. The waves appear huge and menacing from inside the boat. But if you could zoom out to view the entire ocean, you'd notice that those waves are simply little ripples in a much broader pattern.

That is what high-timeframe analysis does for your trading. It offers you perspective. It allows you to remain calm when shorter-term charts are erratic. It keeps you focused on the key decisions that truly matter.

However, high-timeframe analysis is not without its obstacles. One of the most significant is the desire to overtrade. When you see a clear trend on the monthly chart, you may believe that any tiny move is a buying opportunity. Resist the impulse. Remember that these charts change slowly. Before you pull the trigger, wait for clear confirmations.

Another problem is maintaining patience. Monthly charts only provide 12 trading indications per year. The weekly charts provide you 52. When compared to the hundreds or thousands of candles on a daily chart, this is a small number. But it is the goal. Although rare, high-probability setups on high timeframes are frequently worth the wait.

In the following chapter, we'll zoom in and look at daily and 4-hour charts. We'll look at how to apply the context from our high-timeframe analysis to identify high-probability trading opportunities on shorter timeframes. Prepare to bridge the gap between the forest and the trees with your currency analysis.

Chapter 5

Zooming in on daily and 4-hour charts

After viewing the broad vistas of monthly and weekly charts, it's time to restrict our attention. In forex trading, the daily and 4-hour charts are where the real action happens. These timeframes provide an ideal balance between the large picture and the market's minute-by-minute cacophony.

Let's get into the area of intermediate trend analysis.

Intermediate Trend Analysis

Daily charts provide the foundation of many traders' analysis. They offer a balanced perspective of market movements, catching adequate detail but avoiding short-term swings.

For daily chart analysis

- Look for trends that coincide with higher timeframe direction.
- Identify reversal patterns that indicate a shift in the intermediate trend.
- Use daily charts to fine-tune entry and exit positions for long-term trades.

4-hour charts provide more depth, allowing you to see shorter-term trends within the daily movement. They're especially handy for swing traders who maintain positions for a few days or a week.

How to Effectively Use 4-Hour Charts

- Compare 4-hour and daily trends. Are they traveling in unison or divergence?
- Watch for consolidation tendencies that may precede breakouts.
- Use 4-hour charts to optimize entrance time.

Remember that the aim isn't to capture every move. It is to discover high-probability setups that are consistent with the larger picture you've previously constructed across longer timeframes.

Spotting Key Swing Highs and lows

Swing highs and lows are critical pivot moments in the market. They're like signposts, indicating where the market has gone and where it may go.

On daily charts, watch for

- Clear peaks and troughs in price movements.
- Sharp price reversals
- Testing levels numerous times

These swing points frequently serve as crucial support and resistance levels. When the price approaches a prior swing high or low, it's time to pay notice.

On 4-hour charts, you may see smaller swing points amid bigger daily moves. **These can be great for:**

- Establishing more exact stop-loss thresholds.
- Identifying profit-taking opportunities.
- Identifying early signals of trend reversals.

I always highlight major swing highs and lows on my charts. They function as a roadmap of market psychology, indicating where buyers and sellers have historically demonstrated strength.

The Art of Drawing Trendlines

In technical analysis, trendlines are among the most basic yet effective techniques. They work particularly well on daily and 4-hour charts.

How to Draw Effective Trend Lines

- Connect important lows to identify uptrends. Connect major highs to form downtrends.
- Draw a trendline with at least two touch points, ideally three or more.
- A trend line gets more meaningful with more touch points.
- Consider the angle of the trendline. Extremely steep lines are typically unsustainable.
- Trendlines are not just used to identify trends. They can also assist you:
- Identify possible breakouts when price approaches trendlines.
- open position in the direction of the trend.
- Set stop-loss levels below or above the trendline for uptrends and downtrends, respectively.

When trendlines over many timeframes coincide, it is one of the most potent indications in forex trading.

For example, if price is following trendlines on both the daily and 4-hour charts, you've discovered a high-probability setup.

Practical Use of Daily and 4-Hour Analysis:

Now, let's discuss how to use this information to your trading:

Confirm Higher Timeframe Analysis: Use daily charts to corroborate trends from weekly and monthly charts. If they agree, you have a strong preference for your trades.

Identify Entry Points: While higher time frames provide guidance on what to trade, daily and 4-hour charts frequently provide this information. Look for pullbacks as support in uptrends or resistance in downtrends.

Set Realistic Targets: Set realistic profit objectives based on swing highs and lows across specific timeframes. Don't always aim for the moon; accepting profits at reasonable levels might boost your total profitability.

Manage risk: Use these timeframes to define stop-loss thresholds. Set stops beyond recent swing highs or lows, or below/above important trendlines.

Spot Divergences: Identify divergences between price and indicators on specific timeframes. They can detect probable reversals before they appear over longer timeframes.

Monitor Multiple Pairs: Monitor several currency pairings using daily and 4-hour charts. This allows you to identify correlations and divergences between linked pairings.

One of the most difficult aspects of utilizing daily and 4-hour charts is striking the right balance between patience and action. These timeframes provide several possible setups, albeit not all of them will be high-probability trades.

You could notice a gorgeous setup building on the 4-hour chart, only to discover it contradicts the daily trend. Or you can notice a flawless daily chart pattern that contradicts the weekly trend. In these instances, it is typically preferable to wait for alignment across timeframes before entering a trade.

Another problem is to resist the desire to overtrade, it's tempting to believe you should be in a trade all the time. Resist the impulse. Quality setups are worth waiting for.

You'll start to notice the market's rhythm when you add daily and 4-hour analysis into your trading.

You'll observe how prices frequently follow the same levels day after day, and how trends on these timeframes can last for weeks or even months.

You'll also start to understand the market's fractal character. The patterns you observe on daily charts frequently replicate on 4-hour charts, but on a lesser scale. This self-similarity across timeframes is one of the most intriguing elements of FX trading.

Remember that effective trading does not include forecasting the future. It is about recognizing high-probability scenarios and efficiently managing risk. Daily and 4-hour charts provide the tools to accomplish both.

In the following chapter, we'll go deeper into one-hour and shorter timeframes. We'll look at how to utilize these shorter-term charts to make precise inputs and exits while keeping the overall picture in perspective. Prepare to improve your trading abilities and take your analysis to the next level.

Chapter 6

One-Hour and Lower Timeframes

Now we're getting into the thick of things. The action takes place on the 1-hour and smaller timeframes, where trades are won or lost and your nerves are actually challenged. These lower periods are popular among day traders and scalpers, but they are important for all forex traders to grasp.

Let's look at the important components of short-term market structure:

Short-term Market Structure

The 1-hour chart shows how the market's short-term trends and patterns emerge. **This period is ideal for:**

- Identifying intraday trends,
- seeing consolidation patterns and
- Recognizing potential reversal signs.

Keep in mind that:

- short-term patterns may clash with longer-term moves.
- •Price behavior during this interval is more subject to unexpected news developments.
- Higher volatility may occur during key market sessions.

When you look at 15-minute, 5-minute, or even 1-minute charts, you can see the slightest moves in the market. **Here's what you should know:**

- The timeframes are noisy, with many false signals and whipsaws.
- Optimize entry and exit timing.
- Observe market reactions to news events.

I constantly warn traders against depending too much on these smaller periods. It's easy to become caught up in the moment-to-moment swings and lose sight of the broader picture.

Ensure precise entry and exit points

One of the most significant benefits of adopting one-hour and shorter durations is the opportunity to fine-tune your entry and departures. Here's how to efficiently use them:

- To enter, look for pullbacks to support or resistance levels in a bigger trend.
- Consider candlestick patterns to identify potential entry locations.
- Look for breakouts from short-term accumulation patterns.
- To exit, set tight stop-losses based on recent price activity. Use trailing stops to lock in winnings when the trade advances in your favor.
- Look for reversal indications to choose whether to grab winnings.

Remember that accuracy is a two-edged sword. While it might increase your risk-reward ratio, it can also lead to overtrading if not used correctly.

Balancing Big Picture and Immediate Opportunities

This is where the real action in forex trading takes place. You've completed your long-term research for higher periods, but now you're dealing with short-term price activity. How can you strike a balance between the two?

Here is my approach:

- Prioritize higher timeframes. Before you zoom in, be sure you understand the bigger picture.
- Use the 1-hour chart to identify trades that follow the bigger trend.
- Use smaller periods to fine-tune entry and exits.
- When short-term actions clash with long-term trends, proceed with prudence.

It's as if you were a general organizing a fight. The monthly and weekly charts represent your strategic overview. The daily and 4-hour charts represent your tactical strategy. What about the 1-hour and lower timeframes? That's where the actual combat occurs.

Practical Applications of Short-Term Analysis

Now, let's discuss how to use this information to your trading:

Trend Trading: Use the 1-hour chart to identify pullbacks in a wider trend. Then navigate to the 15-minute or 5-minute charts to find your entry.

Breakout Trading: Look for consolidation patterns on 1-hour charts. Use a shorter timeframe to enter as soon as the breakout happens.

Range Trading: Identify range-bound circumstances on higher timeframes. Use the 1-hour and lower charts to trade support-resistance bounces.

News Trading: For successful news trading, smaller timeframes are required. They show you the market's quick response.

Stop Loss Placement: Set exact stop losses using swings on the 15-minute or 5-minute charts.

Take Profit Levels: Set profit goals by analyzing prior support and resistance levels on the 1-hour chart.

Emotional control is one of the most difficult aspects of working within tight time constraints. When you're always following the market, it's easy to succumb to fear and greed. You can enter trades too rapidly or maintain lost positions too long.

That is why, before looking at these charts, you must have a sound trading strategy in place. Prepare your entry criteria, stop loss levels, and profit objectives in advance.

Then, utilize the short-term charts to carry out your strategy rather than making rash judgments.

Another problem is discerning between noise and actual price movement. On a 1-minute chart, even minor wiggles might appear substantial. However, the majority of these changes are simply market noise, or the random back-and-forth between buyers and sellers.

To get through the noise, constantly connect what you're seeing to larger periods. A breakthrough on the 5-minute chart may appear thrilling, but if it is only a little movement inside a bigger range on the 1-hour chart, it may not be as important as you believe.

As you add shorter periods into your research, you'll begin to get a sense of the market's cadence. You'll see how price frequently respects the same levels, even on such short durations. You'll observe patterns that recur fractally throughout timelines.

But don't fall into the trap of believing you can foresee every market movement. Even in the smallest time frames, the market might surprise you. That's why risk management is so important. Never risk more than you can afford to lose on a single trade, regardless of how promising it appears on the 1-minute chart.

Remember that effective trading does not need you to always be correct. It's all about controlling risk and capitalizing on high-probability opportunities. Use these short-term charts to fine-tune your entrances and exits, but keep the overall picture in mind.

In the following chapter, we'll look at how to bring it all together. We'll look at how to mix information from several periods to locate the most likely trades. Prepare to take your forex research to the next level and begin seeing the market in a completely new way.

Chapter 7

Price Action Patterns and Market Structure

Price action patterns serve as the market's language. They are the footprints left by buyers and sellers, revealing a tale about fear, greed, and everything in between. Mastering these patterns is like to learning to read the market's mind.

Let's take a look at price action patterns and how they relate to the overall market structure:

Candlestick Patterns That Matter

Candlesticks are more than simply aesthetically pleasing charts. They depict the conflict between bulls and bears. **Here are a few key patterns to look for:**

Doji: The Doji candle, which indicates uncertainty, might signal a probable reversal, particularly near support or resistance levels.

Doji

Engulfing patterns: A bullish engulfing at support or a bearish engulfing at resistance can be strong reversal signals.

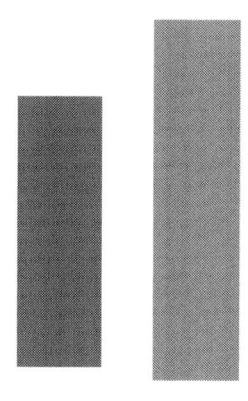

BULLISH ENGULFING

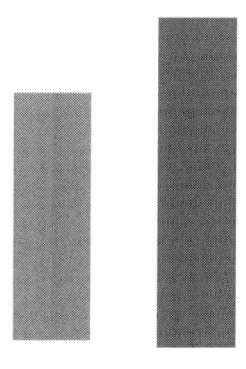

BEARISH ENGULFING

Pin Bars: Pin Bars are rejection candles that show the market believes a price is out of line.

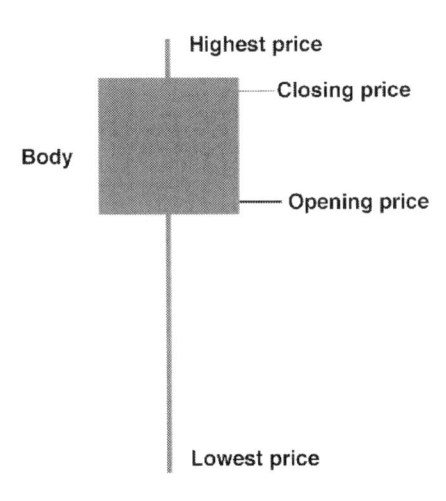

```
                    | Highest price
              ┌─────┤
              │     │──── Closing price
              │     │
      Body ───│     │
              │     │
              │     │──── Opening price
              └─────┤
                    │
                    │
                    │
                    │
                    │ Lowest price
```

Inside Bars: Inside bars indicate consolidation and can lead to large changes.

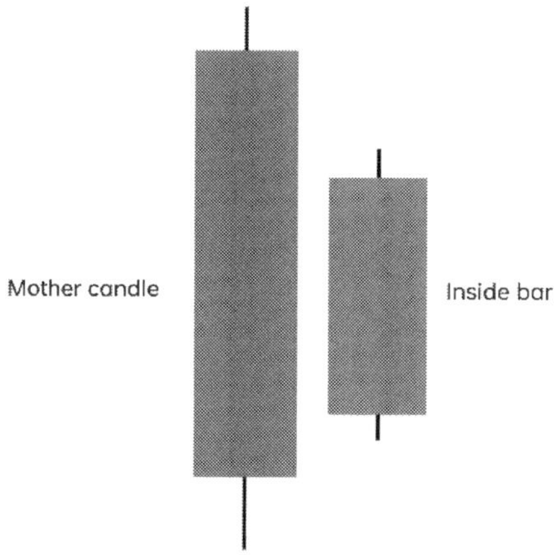
Mother candle
Inside bar

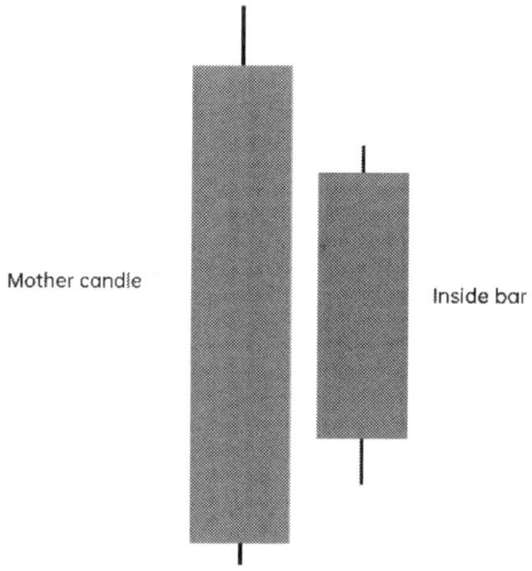
Mother candle
Inside bar

I've discovered that the context for these patterns is critical. A pin bar at a big support level on the daily chart has significantly more significance than one in the middle of nowhere on the 5-minute chart.

Chart Patterns: The Overall Picture

Candlesticks provide short-term information, whereas chart patterns provide a more comprehensive view. They're like road signs, indicating prospective future price fluctuations.

The key chart patterns include:

A reversal pattern known as the Head and Shoulders might signal the conclusion of an uptrend.

Double Tops and Bottoms: These patterns may imply a trend reversal or continuance.

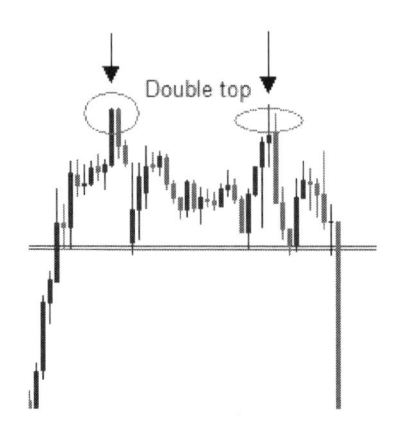

Double bottom

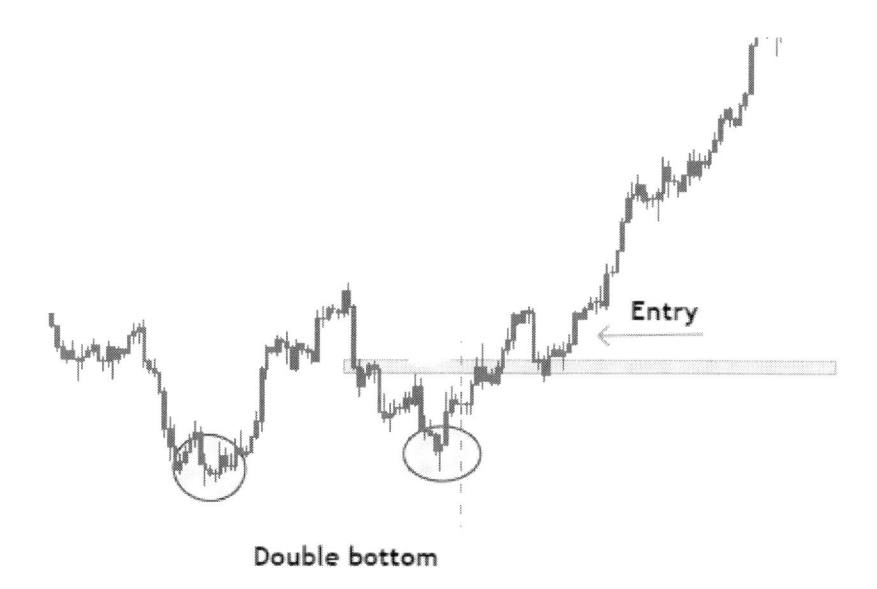

Triangles Pattern: frequently precede big breakouts.

Flags and Pennants: Continuation patterns, like as flags and pennants, can provide fantastic risk-reward trades.

Don't hurry to trade right away when you spot these patterns. Wait for a confirmation. A broken neckline in a head and shoulders, or a breakout from a triangle, might provide more likely setups.

Understanding how patterns fit into the larger market structure

This is when things become interesting. Patterns do not exist in isolation; they are part of the bigger market structure. The key to effective trading is understanding this connection.

Consider the following points:

Trend Context: Bullish patterns in an uptrend are often more trustworthy than those in a downtrend.

Support and Resistance: Support and resistance patterns tend to be more important near key levels.

Multiple Timeframes: A pattern on a higher period might be weighted against a comparable pattern on a lower timeframe.

On the 1-hour chart, you could spot a stunning double bottom.

However, if it is developing at a big resistance level on the daily chart, you should exercise caution. Higher timeframe context may frequently outperform lower timeframe patterns.

Practical Use of Price Action Patterns

Now, let's discuss how to apply these patterns in your trading:

Trend Identification: Identify trends by analyzing broader chart patterns. Head and shoulders or multiple tops/bottoms might signal possible trend reversals.

Entry Timing: Use smaller candlestick patterns to timing your entrance. A pin bar or engulfing pattern at the key level might be a strong entry signal.

Placement of Stop Losses: Set sensible stop losses using the structure of patterns. For example, set a stop below the low of a bullish engulfing pattern.

Take Profit Levels: Use chart patterns to determine profit levels. The height of a triangle extrapolated from the breakout point will help you determine a potential profit objective.

Failure Patterns: Don't disregard when patterns fail. A failing pattern can sometimes result in a powerful shift in the other direction.

Pattern Confluence: Look for patterns that overlap across many timeframes. This convergence can result in high-probability scenarios.

One of the most difficult aspects of trading price action patterns is resisting the want to look for patterns everywhere. Not all double tops are tradeable. Not every doji is a reversal signal. You must be discriminating, concentrating on the clearest, highest-probability scenarios.

Another problem is staying objective. It's easy to slip into the trap of noticing only patterns that support your viewpoint. If you're bullish, you may overlook bearish patterns, and vice versa. Always try to look at the charts with a fresh perspective, challenging your assumptions.

As you include price action patterns into your research, you will begin to perceive the market in a different way. You'll find that some patterns tend to reoccur under various market circumstances. You'll see how the market frequently follows the same levels and patterns over multiple timeframes.

But don't mistake patterns for a crystal ball. They are not assurances of future price movements. These are possibilities, not certainties. That is why risk management is critical, regardless of how flawless a pattern appears.

Remember that effective trading does not include forecasting the future. It is about analyzing current market circumstances and making informed judgments based on probability. Price action patterns are tools to assist you do this, not magic prescriptions for success.

Throughout your trading career, you will discover that some patterns perform better for your style than others. That is okay. The key is to figure out what works for you and improve your talents in those areas. Perhaps you will become an expert at trading flag patterns in trending markets. Perhaps you'll be good at recognizing reversal patterns at key support and resistance levels.

As you practice, you'll gain an almost instinctive understanding of these patterns. You'll see them developing before they're fully developed. You'll get a feel of which ones are likely to succeed and which may fail. This intuition, when paired with sound risk management, may propel your trading to the next level.

In the following chapter, we'll look at how volume influences market structure. We'll look at how the combination of price and volume can give further insights into market activity. Prepare to add another formidable instrument to your trading arsenal.

Chapter 8

Volume and Market Structure

Volume is the secret factor that drives price movement in the currency market. It's like a car's engine: you can't see it, yet it's what propels everything ahead. Understanding volume and its link to market structure can provide you with a considerable advantage in your trading.

Let's look into volume analysis and how it relates to our top-down approach:

Volume Confirms Trends

Volume is the fuel that drives trends. A strong trend should be followed by increased volume. **Here's why it matters:**

- Rising volume in an uptrend indicates increased buyer excitement.

- Increasing volume during a decline suggests increased selling pressure.
- Declining volume in a trend may indicate a probable reversal.

When studying trends, I always focus on volume. It is not only the price direction that matters; the conviction behind the move is as important.

Key points to remember:

- Look for volume spikes at breakout points. High volume breakouts are more likely to be sustained.
- Be cautious of trends that aren't supported by volume. They might be more prone to sudden reversals.
- Volume often leads price. A decrease in volume can signal a trend is losing steam before the price action shows it.

Volume Spread Analysis Basics

Volume Spread Analysis (VSA) is a technique that uses price movement, volume, and spread (the range of each bar) to assess market mood. **Here are some important VSA concepts:**

- High volume with narrow spread: Typically suggests accumulation or dissemination.
- Low volume with wide spread: Low volume and large spread may indicate lack of interest at present price levels.
- High volume with wide spread: High volume and broad spread might foreshadow climactic activity, perhaps leading to reversals.

VSA is very effective at important support and resistance levels. A high volume rejection at a resistance level, for example, might be a powerful negative indicator.

Adding Volume to Your Top-Down Approach

Volume analysis should not exist in isolation. It is most effective when integrated into a larger market structure analysis. Here's how you can accomplish it:

Begin with longer timeframes: Search for major volume patterns on monthly and weekly charts. These might foreshadow key market turning points.

Move to daily charts: Determine how volume interacts with critical support and resistance levels. High volume breakouts or rejections on the daily chart might have important implications.

Fine-tune using intraday charts: Use 4-hour and 1-hour charts to schedule your entry according to volume trends.

Remember that genuine volume data is not available in currency markets, as it is in stocks. We frequently utilize tick volume as a proxy. Although not flawless, it can nevertheless give useful information.

Practical Application of Volume Analysis

Now, let's discuss how to use this information to your trading:

Trend Confirmation: Confirm trends using volume analysis. Strong trends should be supported by increased volume.

Breakout Trading: Identify high volume breakouts from critical levels or chart patterns. These are more likely to persist than low-volume breakouts.

Reversal Identification: Identify reversals by looking for dropping volume in a trend. This might be an early indicator of a probable turnaround.

Support and Resistance: Pay close attention to volume at crucial levels, since high volume rejections can highlight their significance.

Divergences: Identify divergences between price and volume. If the price is reaching new highs but the volume is falling, it may indicate a weakening in the trend.

Climactic Action: High volume might suggest trend tiredness and eventual reversal.

One of the difficulties in employing volume analysis is that it is not always clear. High loudness does not necessarily imply what you believe it does. For example, huge volume at market peaks does not always indicate robust buying; it might represent clever money spreading positions to eager retail traders.

Another issue is the consistency of tick volume in forex. Because we do not have access to genuine volume data, we must be cognizant of the limits of tick volume. It's an effective tool, but it's not flawless.

As you include volume analysis into your trading strategy, you will begin to perceive the market in a new light. When looking at price activity through the prism of volume, it takes on new meaning.

You'll start to comprehend not only what the market is doing, but how dedicated traders are to the move.

You may observe that some support and resistance levels appear to have an almost magnetic impact on price; these levels are frequently connected with strong historical volume. Or you may notice how some trends appear to defy gravity, always reaching new highs or lows; these powerful trends are typically accompanied by continuously growing volume.

But don't mistake volume analysis for a crystal ball. It deals on probabilities rather than certainties, as do other technical analysis techniques. High volume does not ensure a sustained breakout, and low volume does not indicate a trend reversal.

That is why it is critical to incorporate volume analysis into a comprehensive strategy. Combine it with your knowledge of market structure, pricing trends, and fundamental analysis. Look for confluence; when numerous things coincide, you've discovered a high-probability setting.

Remember that effective trading does not need you to always be correct. It is about risk management and taking advantage of high-probability opportunities.

Volume analysis is another tool in your portfolio for identifying opportunities and efficiently managing risk.

Volume analysis may or may not suit your trading style. That is okay. The trick is to explore, practice, and figure out what works best for you. Perhaps you'll become skilled at identifying high-volume breakouts. Perhaps you'll excel at detecting probable reversals using volume divergences.

As you practice, you'll get an almost instinctive sense of how volume relates with pricing. You'll notice when a motion feels "right" depending on the loudness behind it. This intuition, paired with sound risk management and an awareness of market structure, may propel your trading to new heights.

Chapter 9

Fundamental Analysis within the Framework of Market Structure

You can't separate fundamental analysis from market structure. While technical analysis reveals the 'what' of market movements, fundamentals explain the 'why'. Combining these tactics results in a tremendous synergy that may take your trading to new heights.

Let's look at how economic events might change market structure and how to synchronize your technical and fundamental forecasts:

How Economic Events Impact Market Structure

Economic events are the triggers that cause large market movements. They can spark new trends, disrupt current patterns, and even redefine support and resistance levels. **Here's how:**

- Positive economic information can initiate a bullish trend, while bad data may lead to a bearish move.
- Significant news might cause breakouts from consolidation patterns, resulting in new directional moves.
- Support/Resistance movements: Significant economic movements might force price to exceed previously acknowledged levels and establish new ones.

I've seen innumerable examples of how a single economic release may significantly affect the market picture. It's like witnessing an earthquake transform the ground in real time.

Key events to watch:

- Interest rate decisions can have long-term effects on currency values.
- Employment reports can create considerable short-term volatility and indicate economic health.
- GDP data can predict medium to long-term trends.
- Unpredictable geopolitical events might lead to significant market disruptions.

Aligning Fundamental Outlook and Technical Structure

The true power comes from integrating your fundamental and technical analysis. Here's how you can accomplish it:

- Use fundamentals for bias and technicals for timing: Use economic outlook to drive general market views, but use technical analysis for specific entry and exit points.
- When fundamental and technical signs match, it may indicate a high-probability trade situation.
- Resolve conflicts: If fundamental and technical perspectives differ, investigate further. You can be missing an opportunity or a warning sign.

Remember that the market is forward-looking. It frequently pricing in anticipated economic results before they materialize. This is why we occasionally see "buy the rumor, sell the news" circumstances.

Case studies on major fundamental shifts and their technical implications

Let's consider some real-world examples:

Case Study #1: Brexit Vote (2016)

Fundamental Impact: Significant uncertainty for the UK economy.

Technical Implication: The GBP/USD broke key long-term support levels, signaling a significant downtrend.

Lesson: Major geopolitical events can disrupt current technical frameworks.

Case Study 2: Fed Rate Hike Cycle (2015–2018)

Fundamental impact: USD strengthened vs key currencies.

Technical Implication: Resulted in a multi-year rise in the US Dollar Index, with obvious higher highs and lows.

Lesson: Long-term fundamental alterations can lead to consistent trends.

Case Study #3: COVID-19 Pandemic (2020)

Fundamental Impact: The global economic shutdown resulted in significant market volatility.

Technical Implication: Breaking long-term trends and introducing new support/resistance levels across many pairings.

Lesson: Black swan events can totally change market structure over time.

Practical Use of Fundamental Analysis in Market Structure:

Now, let's talk about how to use this information to your trading.

Integrate the economic calendar: to stay on top of important events. These can cause problems in current technical installations.

Conduct Trend Analysis: Use long-term fundamental outlooks to corroborate or challenge observed technical trends.

Support/Resistance Levels: Expect substantial economic events to disrupt long-standing levels. These breakouts might create good trading opportunities.

Prepare for volatility: by adjusting position sizing and implementing stop losses around important news events. Increased volatility might force you out of otherwise profitable trades.

Awareness of Correlation: Recognize how fundamental events in one currency might affect connected pairings.

Track the prevailing market story: When it changes, be ready for potential trend reversals.

Timing is one of the most challenging aspects of integrating fundamental and technical analysis. Fundamentals frequently play out over weeks or months, although technical setups may indicate shorter-term movements. Balancing these many schedules needs experience and patience.

Another difficulty is information overload. With so much economic data accessible, it's easy to become lost in the mix. Focus on the most important events and data points for the currency you're trading.

As you include fundamental analysis into your market structure strategy, you will begin to perceive the forex market in a new light. You'll begin to comprehend not just how the price is moving, but also why.

You may have noticed how some technical levels appear to have an almost mystical capacity to repel price; these levels frequently coincide with crucial fundamental values. Alternatively, you may notice how some trends appear to defy technical analysis, constantly establishing new highs or lows; these moves are typically driven by solid fundamentals.

However, don't believe you can forecast every market move using fundamentals. In the short term, the market might exhibit irrational behavior. That is why combining fundamental analysis with sound technical analysis and risk management is critical.

Remember that effective trading does not need you to always be correct. It is about knowing the market's driving dynamics and making educated decisions based on that information. Fundamental analysis offers another depth to your comprehension, allowing you to make better trading judgments.

During your trading career, you may discover that certain fundamental elements resonate more with your trading style than others. That is okay. The goal is to figure out what works for you and enhance your analysis in those areas. Perhaps you'll become proficient at trading central bank decisions. Or perhaps you'll excel at predicting how geopolitical events will affect currency pairings.

As you practice, you'll get an almost instinctive understanding of how fundamental forces interact with market structure. You will begin to predict how the market will respond to specific sorts of news. This intuition, when paired with sound technical analysis and risk management, may propel your trading to new heights.

Chapter 10

Trading with the trend

Trend trading is frequently regarded as the holy grail of forex trading. It is the skill of aligning with the market's main force and riding the wave of momentum into lucrative trades. However, like any great weapon, it takes talent, patience, and a thorough grasp of market dynamics to be effective.

Let's look at how trend trading fits into our market structure methodology.

Determining the path of least resistance

The first stage in trend trading is to determine which way the market is moving. Sounds simple, right? However, it is more subtle than you may expect.

Trend Identification Key Points:

- Use monthly and weekly charts to identify major trends.
- Confirm many timelines by looking for alignment across them.
- Key level analysis, Trends often follow significant support and resistance levels.

I always begin my trend analysis with greater timeframes. It's similar to gaining a birds-eye perspective of the market landscape. From there, I zoom in to ensure the trend holds up under closer inspection.

Methods for identifying trends

Moving averages: Simple but effective. For uptrends, price should be above the 200-day moving average, while for downtrends, it should be below.

One of the most common definitions of an uptrend is characterized by higher highs and higher lows. Reverse for downtrends.

Use trend-lines: to connect swing lows in uptrends and swing highs in downtrends.

Remember that trends are not always clear-cut. Markets spend a lot of time in consolidation or range-bound mode. Recognizing when a real trend exists is half the fight.

Strategies for Trend Continuation Trading

Once you've recognized a trend, the following step is to locate high-probability entry locations. Here are some strategies to consider.

- For pullback entries, wait for price to retrace to a critical support level in an uptrend (or resistance in a downtrend) before entering.
- For breakout entries, in when price breaks over short-term resistance in an uptrend (or below support in a downtrend).
- Improved average bounces. As dynamic support and resistance at entry locations, use moving averages.

Combining numerous criteria has proven to be a very effective strategy in my experience. For example, a retreat to a major support level that simultaneously corresponds with a moving average might provide as a high-probability entry point.

Entry confirmation techniques:

- Candlestick Patterns: Identify bullish support in uptrends and bearish resistance in downtrends.
- Higher volume entries are more trustworthy.
- Momentum Indicators: RSI and Stochastics can validate trend strength.
- Managing Risk in Trending Markets
- Trend trading may be quite successful, but it is not without risk. Proper risk management is critical.
- Place stop loss orders below recent swing lows in uptrends and above swing highs in downtrends.
- Set a maximum risk to 1-2% of your total balance per trade.
- Use trailing stops to lock in winnings as the trend moves.

Scaling into positions is a risk management method that I swear by. Instead of entering with your whole position size at once, start small and increase as the trend establishes itself.

Risk management tips:

- Be mindful of forthcoming news events that may interrupt the trend.
- Stop chasing the market. If you missed a move, wait for the next one.
- Prepare for trend reversals. There are no trends that stay forever.

Practical Applications of Trend Trading

Now, let's discuss how to use these notions in your trading:

- Procedure for Identifying Trends: Create a regular practice for analyzing trends across several timeframes and currency pairs.
- Create a checklist of required requirements for entering a trend trade.
- For trend trades, aim for a risk-reward ratio of at least 1:2. The high momentum should result in significant profit possibilities.
- Analyze trend strength using indicators such as ADX. Stronger trends are typically more dependable to trade.

- Correlation Awareness: Avoid taking on too many connected trend trades. Diversify across many currency pairs.
- Ensure the fundamental view matches the technological trend. This may boost the likelihood of success.

Patience is one of the most challenging aspects of trend trading. Strong trends do not appear every day, and it is tempting to force trades due to boredom or FOMO (fear of missing out). Remember that sometimes the finest trade isn't really a trade.

Another problem is determining when to depart. It's tempting to hang onto a profitable trade, expecting to milk out every last penny. However, trends may suddenly reverse, and giving up earnings is psychologically difficult.

As you include trend trading into your strategy, you will begin to build an understanding of market momentum. You'll notice when a trend is powerful and sustainable, as well as when it's losing pace.

You may have seen how some trends appear to adhere to specific technical levels with uncanny precision. Or you could notice that some currency combinations trend more clearly than others.

This information comes from experience and may be really useful in your trading selections.

But don't believe that trend trading is easy money. It has ups and downs, as do other trading strategies. There will be false breakouts, surprising reversals, and choppy, trendless markets.

That is why it is critical to combine trend trading with effective risk management and a thorough grasp of market structure. To validate your trend trades, use all available techniques, including price action, volume analysis, and fundamental variables.

Remember that effective trading isn't about timing every move or forecasting the future. It is about manipulating the odds in your favor and successfully managing risk. When done correctly, trend trading may be an effective tool for accomplishing this goal.

Throughout your trading career, you may discover that you have a talent for identifying trends early on, or that you excel at riding long-term trends. The goal is to figure out what works for you and improve your talents in those areas.

Chapter 11

Mastering range-bound markets.

While trend trading receives all of the attention, the truth is that markets spend a large amount of time going sideways. These range-bound situations can be frustrating for trend traders, but understanding them can lead to unusual and profitable possibilities.

Let's see how to navigate and profit from these turbulent waters:

Recognize Consolidation Phases.

The first step in trading ranges is to recognize them. Here's what you should look for:

Price oscillation: Price fluctuates between distinct support and resistance levels.

Lack of Higher Highs/Lower Lows: Ranges don't exhibit continuous directional movement like trends do.

Lower Volatility: Price volatility often decreases inside ranges.

I always start by zooming out of my charts. Sometimes what appears to be a range on the 1-hour chart is really part of a wider trend on the daily chart.

Key range identification techniques:

Support and Resistance Lines: Draw horizontal lines at price reversal levels to indicate support and resistance.

Moving Averages: Flat or criss-crossing moving averages might suggest a range.

Bollinger Bands: Narrowing Bollinger Bands might indicate a consolidation period.

Remember that ranges might exist throughout all timeframes. A 4-hour chart may show a range within a wider daily trend.

Strategies for trading ranges

How do you profit from a range that you've identified? **Here are some strategies to consider:**

- The typical range trading strategy is to buy low and sell high. Buy around support; sell near resistance.
- Enter trades when price fails to break out of a range.
- Middle-Ground Strategies: Use indicators like RSI to trade between oversold and overbought circumstances within a range.

Combining numerous criteria has proven to be a very effective strategy in my experience. For example, buying at support when the RSI is oversold and a bullish candlestick pattern appears.

Range trading tips:

- Be patient. Wait until the price reaches the range's borders before entering.
- Use limit orders to buy near support and sell near resistance.
- Be Aware of Range Contraction: As ranges contract over time, modify targets accordingly.

Breakout Trading: From Ranges to Trends

Every range eventually breaks. When it happens, it can cause major price changes. Here's how you can capitalize on breakouts:

- Identify key levels and know their range bounds.
- Look for Increased Volume: True breakouts are typically accompanied by a jump in volume.
- Strong candles closing beyond the range limit may indicate a breakout.

I usually approach breakouts with a combination of enthusiasm and caution. They can present excellent possibilities, but false breakouts are prevalent.

Strategies for Breakout Trading

- To enter, wait for a candle to close beyond the range.
- Use Stop Orders, Place orders just beyond the range to automatically detect breakouts.
- Be Prepared to Reverse, If a breakout fails, trade the opposite direction.

Practical Application of Range Trading:

Now, let's discuss how to use these notions in your trading:

- Scan your charts on a regular basis for possible range circumstances across various timeframes.

- Create a checklist of criteria for initiating range trades.
- Risk Management: Use tight stop losses in range trades. Because there is no strong directional movement, trades do not require as much space.
- Confirm the range on higher timeframes to prevent trading against major trends.
- Use indicators such as RSI and Stochastic Oscillator to detect overbought and oversold circumstances within the range.
- Breakout Preparation: Plan how to trade probable breakouts from the range.

Boredom is a major difficulty in range trading. The lack of substantial directional movement may entice you to overtrade or push trades that aren't available. Patience is key.

Another problem is determining the difference between a real range and a trend pause. Sometimes what appears to be a range is actually a momentary consolidation before the trend resumes. Multiple timeframe analysis proves to be really useful here.

As you include range trading into your strategy, you'll begin to perceive the market in a different perspective.

You'll start to understand the rhythm of price movements, the ebb and flow of trending and range circumstances.

You may observe that certain currency combinations have a wider range than others. Alternatively, you may see how specific economic situations or times of day are more likely to result in fluctuating markets. This information comes from experience and may be really useful in your trading selections.

However, don't fall into the trap of thinking that range trading is easy money. It has problems, as do other trading strategies. There will be false breakouts, surprise trend resumptions, and times when the range is difficult to identify.

That is why it is critical to combine range trading with sound risk management and a thorough grasp of market dynamics. To validate your range trades and prospective breakouts, use all available tools, including price action, volume analysis, and fundamental variables.

Remember that effective trading isn't about timing every move or forecasting the future. It's all about responding to current market conditions and managing risk efficiently. Range trading, when done correctly, is an effective strategy to profit in markets with no apparent direction.

Throughout your trading career, you may discover that you have a talent for identifying ranges early on, or that you specialize at capturing breakouts. The goal is to figure out what works for you and improve your talents in those areas.

As you practice, you'll develop an almost instinctive feel of when markets are likely to range and when they are about to breakout. As a range approaches its finish, you'll see tension growing, anticipating the possibility of a large shift. This intuition, when paired with thorough research and careful risk management, may make range trading an important part of your forex toolset.

Chapter 12

The Art of Confluence

Confluence in trading is analogous to a perfect storm; when multiple conditions combine, a huge opportunity emerges. It is the result of several diverse analysis approaches working together to point in the same direction. Mastering confluence may significantly improve your trading results.

Let's look at how to integrate multiple timeframes, identify agreement between indicators and price action, and develop a confluence checklist:

Combining many timeframes

Multi-timeframe analysis is a key component of successful trading. Here's how you can put it to use:

Start Big, Go Small: Begin with longer timeframes to gain a better picture, then zoom in for more exact entries.

Look for alignment: When trends converge across multiple timeframes, it sends a powerful signal.

Resolve conflicting timeframes: by investigating the root cause.

I always begin my analysis with the weekly chart, then progress to the daily, 4-hour, and eventually 1-hour charts. This top-down approach keeps me focused on the larger picture.

Key Multi-Timeframe Techniques:

Trend Alignment: Align the trend on your trading period with higher timeframes.

Support/Resistance Confluence: Determine meaningful levels over multiple timeframes.

Entry Confirmation: Confirm entries on lower timeframes to fine-tune those discovered on higher timeframes.

Remember that not all timeframes are created equal. Increase the weight of signals from higher timeframes.

Finding Agreement Between Indicators and Price Action.

Indicators may be strong tools, but they work best when they validate what price action tells you. Here's how you can discover the sweet spot:

- Begin with bare charts and focus on price action. What does price tell you?
- Use selective indicators to avoid cluttering your charts. Select a few crucial indicators that compliment one another.
- Look for convergence. When indicators and price action align, the signal is stronger.

Using momentum indicators to corroborate trend strength demonstrated by price action has proven to be an excellent method in my experience.

Strategies for Indicator Confluence:

Moving Average Convergence: When multiple moving averages line up, it might indicate a strong trend.

Oscillator Agreement: A stronger signal is produced when multiple oscillators (such as RSI and Stochastics) agree.

Volume indicator: Use volume to validate price action.

Creating a Confluence checklist

A confluence checklist can help you objectively assess trading opportunities. **Here's how to make one.**

Identify key factors: List the factors that are most crucial to your trading strategy.

Assign weights: Prioritize the most trustworthy factors.

Establish a Threshold: Determine the number of criteria required for a trade to be considered.

My confluence checklist comprises trend alignment over three timeframes, support/resistance levels, significant indicators, and a fundamental view.

Example confluence checklist:

- Alignment of daily, 4H, and 1H trends.
- Price at important support/resistance levels.
- Candlestick pattern confirms level.
- RSI indicates oversold/overbought.
- Price action is supported by volume.
- 6. The fundamental outlook aligns with the technological picture.

Practical Applications of Confluence

Now, let's discuss how to use these notions in your trading:

- Establish a process to assess markets based on your confluence criteria.
- Journal your trades to identify confluence variables. Over time, you'll discover which are the most dependable.
- Patience is key. Wait for high-confluence setups. It is preferable to miss a trade than to force it with poor confluence.
- Regularly examine and change confluence criteria to reflect market circumstances and performance.
- Risk Management: Consider the strength of confluence while determining position size. Stronger confluence may justify greater holdings.
- Be prepared for outliers. Even with strong confluence, trades can go poorly. Always practice effective risk management.

Analysis paralysis is one of the most difficult problems with Confluence. With so many variables to consider, it's easy to become trapped waiting for the "perfect" configuration.

You must always keep in mind that trading is filled with uncertainty.

Another problem is complicating your analysis. While confluence is effective, there comes a threshold of diminishing returns. Concentrate on the aspects that have proved most helpful for your trading strategy.

As you include confluence into your trading strategy, you will begin to perceive the market in a more holistic light. You will begin to understand how various features of market structure interact and support one another.

You may find that some confluence factors appear to perform better for specific currency pairs or market situations. Alternatively, you could learn that some combinations of elements are more effective. This information comes from experience and may be quite useful in honing your trading skills.

But don't believe that confluence ensures success. It deals on possibilities rather than certainties, as do all parts of trading. Even with significant confluence, there will be some lost trades. That is why risk management is critical.

Remember that effective trading does not need you to always be correct. It's about changing the odds in your favor and properly managing risk. Confluence is a great tool that can help you do this.

During your trading adventure, you may discover that some confluence variables resonate more with your trading style than others. That is okay. The goal is to figure out what works for you and enhance your strategy in those areas.

With practice, you will develop an almost instinctive sense of confluence. You'll begin to see how several elements interact to produce high-probability outcomes. This intuition, when paired with thorough analysis and careful risk management, may propel your trading to new heights.

In the following chapter, we'll look at the crucial topics of risk management and position sizing. We'll look at ways to preserve your capital while increasing your potential rewards. Prepare to understand one of the most important factors of effective Forex trading.

Chapter 13

Risk Management and Position Sizing

Risk management is the foundation for effective forex trading. It's what distinguishes professionals from gamblers. Without it, even the most thorough market study is pointless. Let's look at how to safeguard your capital using correct market structure research, effective stop losses, and sensible position sizing tactics.

Analyzing Market Structures to Protect Your Capital

Market structure research is more than simply locating entry; it's also an effective risk management tool. Here's how.

Identify key levels: Use support and resistance to determine reasonable stop loss locations.

Recognize Volatility: The volatility profiles of various market configurations vary. Adjust your risk appropriately.

Recognize potential reversals: Recognize early signals of trend shifts to safeguard your earnings.

I always begin my risk assessment by looking at the larger picture. What does the entire market structure suggest about potential risks?

Key risk management approaches based on market structure:

- Place stop loss orders on longer timeframes.
- Be cautious while trading against strong trends.
- Adjust position sizes to reflect market structure.

Remember that your first responsibility as a trader is to safeguard your capital. Without it, you will be unable to continue playing.

Setting stop losses based on structure

Stop losses are a safety net. They should be set at levels that, if reached, will show your trade notion incorrect. Here's how to apply market structure to stop loss placement:

- Use the Swing Point Method to place stops beyond the most recent swing highs and lows.
- Use the Structure Break Method to set stops at levels that would invalidate the existing market structure.

- Utilize tools such as Average True Range (ATR) to create stops based on market volatility.

Combining different strategies has shown to be a successful approach in my experience. For example, set a stop beyond a swing point but no closer than 1 ATR from my entry.

Stop-loss strategies:

- Set a stop loss before beginning a trade.
- Avoid establishing stops at apparent levels where other traders may place theirs.
- Use a time stop on trades that don't move in your favor after a set period.

Position Sizing Strategies for Various Market Conditions

When it comes to risk management, position sizing is critical. It calculates how much you stand to make or lose from each trade. Here's how to tackle it:

- Risk a preset proportion of your account on each trade.
- Adjust position size based on market volatility.

- Use confidence-based sizing to increase size for high-confidence setups and decrease size for lower-confidence trades.

I usually use a combination of these methods, beginning with a base risk percentage and changing according to volatility and trade confidence.

Tips for position sizing:

- Never risk more than one or two percent of your account on a single trade.
- Reduce position sizes during turbulent or uncertain markets.
- Grow your account gradually, rather than suddenly.

Practical Application of Risk Management:

Now, let's discuss how to use these notions in your trading:

Pre-Trade Checklist: Create a checklist that includes a risk assessment before each trade.

Risk/Reward Ratio: Aim for a minimum risk-reward ratio of 1:2 on each trade.

Drawdown Rules: Set the maximum drawdown amounts for your account. If you attain your goal, take a step back and rethink your plan.

Regularly review your trades: Do you adhere to your risk management guidelines?

Before entering a trade: examine several situations. What are your plans if the market goes against you?

Emotional Control: Accept that effective risk management frequently involves missing out on trades. That is okay.

Emotional control is one of the most challenging aspects of risk management. It's tempting to shift stop losses, raise position sizes after a loss, or break the rules in the heat of the moment. The key to success is discipline.

Another problem is balancing risk and return. Too cautious, and your earnings may be insufficient to balance losses. Too aggressive, and a few poor trades might wipe out your account. Finding the correct balance requires time and expertise.

As you use these risk management techniques to your trading, you will begin to perceive the market differently. You'll start to think in terms of risk first and return second.

This transformation in mentality is critical to long-term success.

Some traders appear to flourish in tumultuous environments, while others favor tranquil markets. Alternatively, you may realize that some sorts of trades have consistently higher risk-reward profiles for your trading style. This self-awareness develops with experience and may be quite useful in improving your approach.

But don't fall into the trap of believing that faultless risk management ensures success. There will continue to be losing streaks and drawdowns. The aim is not to prevent all losses, but to guarantee that no single defeat (or series of losses) would force you out of the game.

Remember that effective trading does not need you to be right all of the time. It is about managing risk properly so that your wins outperform your losers over time. Good risk management allows you to withstand the inevitable ups and downs of FX trading.

During your trading adventure, you may discover that certain risk management approaches connect better with your personality than others. That is okay. The key is to develop a method that you can follow consistently, even when circumstances get rough.

With experience, you'll acquire an almost intuitive sense of risk. You'll develop an intuition for when a trade is too hazardous or when market conditions necessitate greater care. This intuition, paired with thorough study and focused execution, can be the difference between long-term success and failure in forex trading.

Chapter 14

Building Your Trading Plan

A trading plan is your own road map to forex success. It represents the conclusion of everything we've talked, suited to your specific objectives and circumstances. Without a proper plan, you're simply another ship lost in the great expanse of the currency market.

Let's go over how to develop a complete trading plan that combines market structure analysis into your daily routine:

Incorporate Market Structure Analysis into Your Daily Routine

Consistency is essential in forex trading. Here's how to turn market structure analysis into a daily habit:

- Create a schedule, Set aside specified hours each day for market analysis.

- Begin with broad timeframes and narrow them down.
- Use checklists, Develop a step-by-step procedure for your analysis.

I always begin my day with a general market review before focusing on individual currency pairings. This allows me to keep focused on the bigger picture.

A daily analysis practice involves:

- Reviewing key economic events and news,
- Analyzing long-term patterns on weekly and daily charts.
- Identify critical support and resistance levels.
- Search for probable trade setups.

Remember that your schedule should reflect your lifestyle and trading style. A day trader's schedule will be considerably different from a swing trader's.

Develop a Top-Down Analysis Template.

A template simplifies your analysis procedure, preventing you from missing important tasks. **Here's how to make one:**

Define your timeframes: Decide which timeframes you will evaluate on a regular basis.

List key elements: Include trend analysis, support and resistance levels, indicators, and so forth.

Create a visual aid Use screenshots or drawings to show what you're searching for.

My strategy begins with monthly charts for the general trend, then progresses to daily charts for significant levels, and finally 4-hour and 1-hour charts for prospective entry.

Example template structure:

- Conduct monthly or weekly trend analysis.
- Medium-term market structure (daily).
- Short-term opportunity (4H/1H).
- Key levels and probable trade opportunities.
- Calculate risk and position size.
- Recording and reviewing your trades.

A trading log serves as your own personal feedback loop. It is how you learn from your accomplishments and errors. **Here's how to make the best of it:**

- Keep detailed records of all trades, including reasons, emotions, and market circumstances.
- Be honest about your faults and triumphs.

- •Review regularly: Set aside time every week or month to review your trades.

I find that examining my journal allows me to identify trends in my trading that I might otherwise overlook.

- Trade information (entry, exit, position size, etc.)
- Screenshots of the setup
- Your analysis and rationale
- Results and lessons learned

Practical Applications of Your Trading Plan:

Now, let's discuss how to put your plan into action.

- Start small: Test your plan with paper trading or tiny holdings.
- Maintain Consistency: Stick to your plan, even if it's tempting to depart.
- Regularly review and adjust your plan to ensure its efficacy.
- Stay accountable by sharing your plan with a mentor or trading companion for feedback.
- Utilize technology: Use trading notebooks and analysis tools to streamline your approach.

- Continuously educate yourself on market structure and trading tactics.

Staying disciplined is one of the most difficult aspects of developing and sticking to a trading plan. When things are going well, sticking to your plan is simple; but, during losing streaks or turbulent markets, it becomes much more difficult.

Another problem is achieving the appropriate mix of structure and flexibility. Your plan should be thorough enough to guide your selections while also being adaptable to shifting market conditions.

As you follow your trading plan, you will see trends in your trading behavior. You may find that you do better at various times of day or with specific currency combinations. Alternatively, you may realize that certain components of market structure analysis are more compatible with your trading style than others.

You could discover that certain aspects of your plan perform better than others. Maybe your long-term trend analysis is correct, but your short-term entry timing need improvement. Perhaps your analysis is sound, but your risk management has to be tighter.

This self-awareness is crucial. It enables you to constantly improve your approach, capitalizing on your strengths while bolstering your deficiencies.

However, do not fall into the trap of frequently modifying your plans. Give it time to work. Trading is a probabilistic game performed across a large number of trades. A few defeats do not always indicate that your plan is incorrect.

Remember that a trading plan isn't a prison sentence. It's a framework for making smarter judgments and managing risk effectively. It should change as you progress as a trader, but the fundamental fundamentals, such as sound market structure analysis and risk management, should remain consistent.

During your trading adventure, you will most likely go through multiple versions of your trading plan. That is normal. As you get more experience and a better grasp of market structure, your plan will organically adapt.

As you practice, you'll gain an almost instinctive understanding of how to apply your plan to various market circumstances. You'll begin to distinguish circumstances in which tight adherence to the plan is required and others in which a little flexibility may be useful.

A mature trader maintains a combination of discipline and flexibility. It requires expertise, self-reflection, and a thorough grasp of both the markets and your own trading mentality.

In the next chapter, we will look at some advanced topics in market structure analysis. We'll look at how order flow, market profile, and other advanced features may enhance your trading experience. Prepare to advance your market structure analysis to the next level.

Chapter 15

Advanced Concepts of Market Structure

As your trading adventure progresses, you will come across increasingly complicated tools and concepts. These advanced techniques can deepen your market structure analysis, providing fresh insights and trading possibilities. Let's look at some of these cutting-edge techniques.

Order Flow and Market Structure

Order flow analysis is similar to gazing into the market's inner workings. It's about understanding the buying and selling pressures that drive price changes. Here's how it affects market structure:

Identify Key Levels: Order flow can disclose hidden levels of support and opposition.

Spotting Reversals: Large orders at specific prices might indicate probable trend shifts.

Understanding Momentum: Order speed and magnitude might reflect market strength.

I've discovered that combining order flow and standard market structure analysis may be really effective. It's like incorporating a third dimension into your charts.

Important order flow concepts:

- Absorption occurs when big orders are filled without major price changes.
- Sweeps are rapid price moves that clear numerous price levels.
- Iceberg Orders are large orders that are hidden from the order book and only exposed once they are filled.

Remember that order flow analysis necessitates specific tools and data streams. A normal charting software cannot accomplish this.

Using Market Profile and Structure Analysis

Market Profile is a distinct method of viewing price and time correlations. It can provide new insights into market structure.

- **Identify Value Areas:** Determine the market's primary focus.
- **Monitor balance and imbalance:** to identify possible breakout opportunities.
- **Multiday Profiles:** Gain insight into market structure over time.

One method that I've found successful is to use Market Profile to validate significant levels detected by traditional structure analysis.

Market Profile Applications:

Identify Fair Value: To determine fair value, use the Point of Control (POC) to discover balanced price levels.

Spot Failed Moves: When prices cannot hold beyond the value region, they commonly return to it.

Understand Trader mood: The profile shape indicates bullish or bearish mood.

Fibonacci Levels and Their Impact on Market Structure

Fibonacci retracements and extensions can improve the precision of your market structure analysis.

- Fibonacci levels frequently correspond with conventional support and resistance (S/R).
- Use Fibonacci to assess trend strength and identify probable reversals.
- Harmonic Patterns: Advanced Fibonacci linkages can create tradeable patterns.

I usually overlay Fibonacci levels on my charts once I've identified major swing points. It's astonishing how frequently pricing follows these mathematical correlations.

Trading Methods Using Fibonacci

- Use Fibonacci retracements to identify entry points in trending markets.
- Set profit objectives with Fibonacci extensions.
- Confluence Trading: Identify trades where several Fibonacci levels align with other technical considerations.

Practical use of advanced concepts:

Now, let's talk about how to use these advanced techniques to your trading.

Begin slowly: Don't try to incorporate all these notions simultaneously. Include them one at a time in your analysis.

Demonstrate the techniques: They can be sophisticated. Prior to utilizing real money, practice on a demo account.

Combine with Basics: Maintain your basic analysis. Use these advanced principles to supplement, not replace, your primary strategy.

Be selective: Not all advanced techniques are suitable for your trading style. Find out what works for you.

Continuous Learning: These disciplines are complex. Commit to continuing your studies to master them.

Seek Mentorship: Find a mentor who has experience with these advanced techniques.

One of the most difficult obstacles in embracing advanced concepts is information overload. With so much information accessible, it's easy to become overwhelmed with analysis. Remember that the purpose is to improve your decision-making, not confuse it.

Another difficulty is the tendency to detect patterns everywhere. Just because you can draw Fibonacci numbers or comprehend a Market Profile does not imply that every occurrence is marketable. Maintain your discipline and trading guidelines.

As you use these advanced principles, you will begin to perceive the market in new ways. You may notice that particular Fibonacci levels frequently serve as turning points in your preferred currency pairings. Alternatively, you may realize that order flow analysis provides you an advantage in determining the end of retracements.

Market Profile may help you comprehend the long-term structure of the markets in which you trade, providing context for your short-term actions. Perhaps you'll acquire a talent for identifying high-probability settings in which many advanced indications agree with your traditional analysis.

This better awareness can be exciting, but it also has hazards. It's easy to fall into the trap of believing you can foresee every market movement. Remember that even with the most advanced analysis, the market can still surprise you.

That is why it is critical to have a strong foundation in risk management and fundamental market structure analysis. These advanced techniques should improve your trading, not replace basic concepts.

You will most likely experience both exhilaration and frustration while learning these advanced ideas. That is normal. Some days, everything seems to click, and you feel as if you've discovered the market's secrets. On other days, these techniques may appear unduly complicated or untrustworthy.

As you practice, you will get an instinctive understanding of when and how to use these advanced principles. You'll begin to recognize circumstances when order flow analysis might provide you a competitive advantage, or when a certain Fibonacci connection is likely to be relevant.

This intuition, when paired with a solid understanding of market structure and rigorous risk management, may propel your trading to new heights. However, it demands patience, perseverance, and a dedication to lifelong learning.

In the last chapter, we will look at the future of forex trading. We'll look at evolving technology, how to react to shifting market dynamics, and the value of constant learning in your trading path. Get ready to peek into the forex trading crystal ball and prepare for the difficulties and possibilities that await you.

Chapter 16

The Future Of Forex Trading

The forex market is constantly developing, influenced by technical advancements, global events, and alterations in trading paradigms. As we approach a new age in trading, it is critical that we look forward and prepare for the changes that are coming.

Analysis of emerging technologies in the market.

Technology is transforming the way we analyze and trade the forex market. Here are some crucial developments to monitor:

AI and Machine Learning: These technologies are improving their pattern detection and predictive analysis capabilities.

Big Data Analytics: Processing large volumes of data provides valuable insights into market behavior.

Blockchain and Cryptocurrencies: Blockchain and cryptocurrency technologies are impacting forex trading and might transform the global financial environment.

I'm particularly interested about AI's ability to spot intricate market structures that human traders may overlook. However, these technologies must be approached critically.

Considerations for new technologies:

- Integration with Traditional Analysis: How can new technology complement traditional market structure analysis?
- Ethical implications: Evaluate the fairness and transparency of AI-driven trading systems.
- Stay up-to-date on regulatory changes in response to emerging technologies.

Remember that technology should improve, not replace, your trading knowledge and decision-making abilities.

Responding to shifting market dynamics.

The forex market is continually developing. Here's how to remain ahead:

Global Economic Shifts: Monitor global economic shifts and their influence on currency relationships.

Evolving trading instruments: New products, such as forex options and exotic pairings, are offering new opportunities.

Changing trading hours: Traditional trading sessions are becoming less clear as global markets grow increasingly integrated.

Reassessing my market assumptions on a frequent basis is one method that has been helpful for me. What was successful last year may not be effective in the future.

Tips for responding to market changes:

- Stay informed about global economic news and policy developments.
- Be flexible and alter your trading approach when market conditions change.
- Diversify Your Skills: Avoid relying on a single trading strategy. Create a diversified skill set.

Continuous learning and improvement.

In the fast-paced world of forex trading, staying steady means falling behind. Here's how to continue growing:

- Formal Education: Consider taking additional courses or certificates in forex trading and financial markets.
- Connect with other traders through forums, meetings, or trading groups to learn from their experiences.
- Review and analyze your trades to discover areas for improvement.

I make it a point to spend time each week studying new things about the markets. It may be a new analysis approach, a thorough dive into a currency pair, or trying out a new trading platform.

Strategies for Continuous Improvement:

- Set Learning Goals: Clearly define your learning objectives.
- Demonstrate new strategies or techniques on a demo account before adopting them in actual trading.

- Seek Mentorship: Connect with experienced traders to aid your progress.

Practical Application to Future-Proof Your Trading:

Now, let's talk about how to plan for the future of forex trading:

- Integrate technology to improve market structure analysis, including AI and big data.
- Diversify your skills to avoid relying just on one. Develop abilities in a variety of trading strategies and analysis techniques.
- Stay informed, follow financial news and market updates regularly.
- Networking, build relationships with other traders and industry professionals. Knowledge exchange is essential in this profession.
- Embrace change and be open to new ideas and ways. Tomorrow's markets may alter significantly from those of today.
- Ethical Consideration, as trading gets increasingly automated, think about the ethical implications of your trading strategies.

One of the most difficult difficulties in planning for the future of forex trading is information overload. With so many new technologies and strategies developing, it is easy to become overwhelmed. The goal is to concentrate on comprehending fundamental ideas that will endure regardless of technical advancements.

Another problem is striking the right balance between innovation and tried-and-true approaches. While it is critical to accept new technologies and techniques, do not abandon tried-and-true approaches to market structure analysis. The principles we've examined throughout this book are likely to stay relevant for many years to come.

As you negotiate the changing environment of forex trading, you will undoubtedly face times of exhilaration and worry. You could find that AI technologies provide fantastic insights into market structure, or that conventional analysis mixed with new data sources provides you an advantage.

You might find yourself trading currency pairings or derivatives that do not yet exist. Alternatively, you may design strategies that combine high-frequency algorithmic trading with long-term fundamental analysis.

This trip into the future of forex trading might be exciting, but it also has hazards. It's easy to get caught up in the buzz around new technologies or trading strategies without fully comprehending the repercussions.

That is why it is critical to have a strong foundation in risk management and market structure analysis. Even as our technologies get more complex, the fundamental principles of supply and demand, trend analysis, and risk management are likely to remain important.

On your path to the future of forex trading, you will most likely experience times of quick learning and adaptability. That is normal. Some days, you'll feel like you're at the forefront of trading technology. Other days, you may feel as if you're trying to keep up with the rate of change.

As you continue to study and adapt, you'll have an instinctive understanding of which new innovations are actually game-changing and which are merely fleeting fads. You'll begin to see how developing technologies may enhance, rather than replace, your grasp of market structure.

The key to long-term success in forex trading is to strike a balance between embracing innovation and building a solid foundation. It necessitates curiosity, adaptability, and a dedication to lifelong learning.

Conclusion

As we near the finish of our adventure through the complex world of forex trading and market structure analysis, it's time to pause and reflect on the route we've taken together. This book has been a thorough examination of the art and science of interpreting market movements, from the broad strokes of long-term trends to the small details of short-term price action.

Let's summarize some of the main things we've discussed:

We began by studying the fundamentals of market structure, including how to spot trends, support and resistance levels, and critical swing points. These are the fundamentals of any successful trading strategy, the ABCs of the forex language. If you just remember one thing from this book, it's that the market is continuously giving us a tale. Our duty as traders is to learn how to understand that tale and make sound judgments based on what we observe.

We then discussed the effectiveness of top-down analysis, which has saved my bacon more times than I can count.

Starting with the large view over longer timeframes and then focusing in provides context that can help us avoid rookie mistakes. I can't tell you how many times I've been tempted to do a trade based on a 15-minute chart, only to zoom out and see it contradicts a huge weekly trend. That's the beauty of top-down analysis: it keeps you accountable.

The price action patterns were next on our target list. We investigated how candlestick forms and chart patterns might provide insights into market psychology. Remember that these patterns aren't magic bullets; they're signals that must be validated by further elements. But when you see a gorgeous head and shoulders pattern emerging at a major resistance level, and volume confirms the move, trading becomes thrilling.

We also discussed the frequently ignored subject of volume in Forex trading. While we do not have genuine volume data in forex like we do in stocks, tick volume can nevertheless give useful information. I've discovered that combining volume analysis and price movement may provide you a significant advantage, particularly when confirming breakouts or spotting potential reversals.

Fundamental analysis was another important issue we discussed. In my early trading career, I was just a technical analyst. I believed news and economic statistics were simply noise. Boy, was I mistaken. Learning to blend basic and technical analysis was a game changer for me. It's like having a map and a compass: technical analysis shows you where you are, while fundamental analysis explains why you're there and where you could be going.

We also got into the details of trend trading and range trading. These are two sides of the same coin, and understanding them can help you become a more flexible and lucrative trader. I remember when I initially started out, I was always looking for trends. It took me a long to realize the beauty (and profit potential) of well-defined range markets.

Risk management and position sizing are possibly the most significant subjects in this book. I cannot emphasize this enough: you can be correct about market direction 90% of the time, but if your risk management is inadequate, you will still blow up your account. Believe me, I learnt this lesson the hard way early in my career. Proper risk management is not glamorous, but it is what keeps you in the game long enough to be lucrative.

We concluded by discussing advanced principles and future trends in forex trading. The trading industry is fast developing, with artificial intelligence and big data analytics altering the game. But here's the thing: no matter how smart our technologies develop, the fundamental concepts of market structure and pricing action will remain valid. The tools may evolve, but the basic market dynamics stay constant.

You could be feeling overwhelmed right now. That is normal. Forex trading is a tough topic, and we've covered a lot of material. But remember, you don't have to master everything at once. Trading is an experience, not a place you get to.

When I initially started trading, I tried every strategy and indicator I came across. It was a mess. I was very analytical and second-guessed every trade. Things didn't start to make sense until I took a step back, concentrated on mastering a few key principles, and truly understood market structure.

So, my recommendation to you is to start easy. Concentrate on comprehending trends, support and resistance levels, and fundamental price action patterns. Practice spotting them on charts with varying times.

To test your analysis without risking real money, trade on paper or with a demo account.

As your confidence grows, progressively introduce more sophisticated topics. Perhaps you'll discover that Fibonacci retracements are particularly suitable for your trading strategy. Perhaps you'll develop a flair for trading breakouts. The idea is to uncover what works for you and keep refining your strategy.

Keep in mind that there is no one best trading strategy. No one strategy or indicator can ensure consistent profitability. Success in forex trading requires a thorough grasp of market dynamics, a sound trading strategy, and the discipline to stick to it.

It's also important to recognize that lost trades are all part of the game. Even the most successful traders in the world do not win every trade. What distinguishes great traders is their ability to manage risk and limit their losses while allowing their winnings to run.

Continue to be interested and learn as you progress through your trading career. The market is always changing, and so should you. Attend seminars, study books, and join trading groups.

However, you should always approach your learning critically. Not every strategy or approach will suit your trading style or risk tolerance.

Finally, have patience with yourself. Becoming a consistently profitable forex trader requires time. There will be highs and lows, times of clarity and bewilderment. It's all part of the process. What important is that you remain devoted to your own development and learning.

Access Your Forex Trading Videos!

Thank you for reading! As a special offer for purchasing this book, you can access exclusive forex trading videos designed to boost your knowledge and skills.

To get your videos, simply follow the link below:

subscribepage.io/jidegeorge

You can copy and paste the link into your browser or type it directly to access the videos.

Here's the link again:

subscribepage.io/jidegeorge

Printed in Great Britain
by Amazon